I0191924

Anonymous

The Shadow and the Cloud

Anonymous

The Shadow and the Cloud

ISBN/EAN: 9783337340520

Printed in Europe, USA, Canada, Australia, Japan

Cover: Foto ©Lupo / pixelio.de

More available books at **www.hansebooks.com**

Sh?dow ... nd.

Entered according to Act of Congress, in the year 1870, by the
STANDARD LIFE INSURANCE COMPANY, in the Clerk's
Office of the District Court of the United States,
for the Southern District of New York.

E. J. PECK, Printer, 65 Liberty St., N. Y.

The Shadow in the Valley.

"OH! has the doctor come yet? So moaned out a feverish invalid, waking up from a brief, uneasy sleep, or rather delirium, in which he had been groaning and tossing restlessly from side to side of his bed, like some wild animal dashing himself against the bars of his cage.

"The doctor," said his pale wife, coming from the window, where she had gone to weep unobserved, "why, it is only half an hour since he was here and told you he would not be back for three hours. What can I do for you?"

"Slept only half an hour! It seemed like two days. I had such dreams. I saw spectres worse than Dante's Inferno."

"What were they like?"

"Oh, I was walking among large handsome buildings, when suddenly their fronts fell off and left the timbers exposed. And on every timber, from the ground to the roof, were crowed hideous negroes, staring and leering and grimacing at me as they hung thickly upon the beams, twisting themselves over one another's heads to climb up higher to some vacant notch, where they could better rivet their great glaring eyes on me. They looked like devils incarnate, with a family likeness.

"Then I was in a great gallery of paintings of the old masters. Noble, grey-haired men and women looked down upon me out of their frames. But when I turned my eyes away, the portraits changed to sneering, malicious faces, whose eyes followed me with a mocking, ghastly smile. If I turned and fixed upon them a steady gaze I could bring back the original face. But when I again passed on, back the impish satanic leer would come, till I saw by side glances that the whole gallery was so, except just the one face I had before my eyes. And all those faces looked alike.

"Poor, dear husband," exclaimed his wife, grasping his hand. "It is your fever. Don't think about those things any more."

"Oh! I knew they were dreams. Next, I was in a large theatre, floored over for a hall, and the floor was filled with men standing half-turning, crouching, stooping, bending, all immovable and all looking fixedly at me with a solemn, warning look. As I watched them, they all suddenly changed to different figures in new attitudes, but occupying the same place as before, and still keeping their eyes fixed upon me. And so again and again did they change, instantaneously, without a figure having moved from the spot where he stood, or taking his steady gaze one moment from my face. And in the features of all there was a terrible similarity, suggesting some person whom I cannot recall—unless it be———but no matter."

The wife was shocked by these fearful images of a distorted fancy. " Here," she said, " let me turn your pillow and bathe your forehead. Take some of these soothing drops, and try to sleep and think of pleasanter things."

Still the sick man continued : " Then I saw a frozen human body floating on an icy desert sea ; where all was so bleak and dreary and still, that even the wind and the air seemed frozen, and the sky looked a dull, chill grey, and the only moving thing was the dead body, rocked on its icy bed. And so I watched this frozen corpse to see if it were mine, for a long day and night. Night or day made little difference in that awful scene. That vision haunts me yet. For I thought that man had lived a selfish life, and he had let his heart grow so cold that he was to be frozen, body and soul, forever and forever,—frozen—forever—and forever—frozen.

" I will sit by you, George," said his loving wife, "and hold your hand in mine, and then, perhaps, you can rest more quietly. The doctor says you must sleep."

Soon again the sufferer slept, but it was still in a troubled, uneasy way. His faithful nurse sat by him and sought to soothe his slumbers by every device her love could suggest, but in vain. Still he tossed restlessly to and fro, muttering words, among which his wife distinguished sometimes her own name, and sometimes that of the children, and once the words, "My poor wife—poor Willie and Ella!" pronounced in such a sorrowful, self-reproachful tone, and accompanied with such groans of agony that she felt compelled to arouse him from his slumbers.

When the doctor came he was alarmed at the delirious state of his patient. He had expected to find him more quiet from the powerful opiates he had left. The increasing delirium was a dangerous sympton. He said:

" You must keep him quiet, send the children away to your friends, close the blinds, deaden the noise on the pavements in front with straw, keep ice on his head and double the dose of drops. I shall be back in two hours."

The wife followed the doctor out of the room and asked him tremblingly his real opinion of her husband's condition. He hesitated a moment and said :

" While there is life there is hope. I do not like the continued high fever. Your presence, strange to say, excites him. You had best not remain in the room. He appears to have some trouble on his mind."

"I cannot see what it can be doctor; he has no secrets from me."

"Well, to minister to a mind diseased is not my province. I should recommend you to send for his clergyman. Perhaps a talk with him might unburden your husband's mind and do him good. I don't believe in their interference with sick men generally. That sort of thing often does more harm than good, but in this case I should try it."

Through the long watches of that night the sick man continued in a half conscious delirium, and the devoted wife sat behind the curtains of the bed and watched his sufferings, unable to give relief.

In the morning the clergyman came, a sincerely pious man, devoted to his labors among the sick. The patient was weaker and quieter. He seemed somewhat benefitted by the reading and praying of the goodman; but it was rather as a pleasing distraction than anything else, until the clergyman, to arouse his mind, read the twenty-fifth chapter of Matthew.

When they came to the words, "I was hungry and ye gave me food, thirsty and ye gave me drink, naked and ye clothed me, &c.," he started, fixed his eyes intensely upon the reader, and begged a repetition of the words; this done, he sighed deeply and asked :

" Whom is a man most bound to provide for ; his family or others ? "

" His family, of course," was the reply.   " But he should not indulge his family in immoderate luxuries and so prevent himself from giving to the poor the necessaries of life."

" I *mean* the necessaries of life, bread, clothing, and shelter," replied the sick man, speaking with terrible earnestness.

The clergyman gave a glance around the room, upon the elegant furniture and the many articles of expensive taste, and his looks said plainly that he considered that supposition an improbable one.   He thought the invalid's mind was wandering.

" No, sir," said the sick man, with a hollow tone. " If I die to-day, my family to-morrow will not have the right to bread for their hunger, nor to a roof to shelter them from the cold and the storm.   To pay my debts will take everything I have, and my poor wife and children will be left homeless and penniless, —perhaps friendless."   And the invalid sank back upon his pillow and pressed his hand to his forehead.

The minister was surprised at the statement, but proceeded to administer the usual consolations: " The Lord will provide.   He tempers the winds to the shorn lamb.   Look at the lilies of the valley, &c. The sparrows of the field, &c.," and so forth.

"Yes, but the poor lambs suffer for all that. And I have seen the lilies crushed by the heavy foot of the careless passer-by, and the sparrow dead upon the hard frozen ground. And I have seen," sinking his voice to a whisper, "the widow and the fatherless pinched by hunger and the winter's cold,—and it has made my heart bleed. But oh, heavens! I never thought my own would drag out a living death of that kind. My darling wife, my dear children, beggars! Respectable, starving, beggars! Will they grow strong and hearty by hardships, or will they not sink under the rough change? Will not their sensitive natures be crushed by the fearful conflict; or, worse, will their hearts not grow callous and morose?"

Here the clergyman again saw an excellent opening for scriptural comforts and so immediately replied:

"Whom the Lord loveth, He chasteneth" "Tribulation worketh patience," and so on.

"I cannot be comforted by that. I think that even if it needs be that these things come, still woe unto me by whom they have come. I have been a thoughtless, careless, man, led a butterfly existence —I could have provided for my family against my sudden death by a Life Insurance Policy, but I put it off and put it off—I am feeling all the tortures of remorse for my unfeeling conduct—and oh, will not

my wife and children feel like cursing my name in-
stead of remembering it with affection. Why, why
did I not provide for this risk of an early death!
Why did not some friend, why did not *you* tell me
this was my duty. You preached about death and
about being good to the poor; but you never warned
me that the poor might be those of my own house-
hold. I hear that sentence ringing in my ears :
" You have not clothed the naked, you have not fed
the hungry, depart from me ye worker of iniquity !"

The clergyman insisted, " Sir, it seems that your
heart still clings, in the hour of death, to the flesh-
pots of Egypt. Do you not know that riches profit-
eth nothing." "Blessed be ye poor." " Blessed
are ye that hunger now."

The sick man rose it his bed, supporting himself
with difficulty in a sitting posture by his arms
braced behind him, and with wasted sunken cheeks
but eyes glittering with fever he poured forth a tor-
rent like this :

" You misapply scripture. It was there meant
poverty of the spirit, hungering after righteousness.
I tell you money is one of God's means of doing good.
Woe to him who squanders his talent. You pray for
the *souls* of the heathen ; can you reach their souls
without elevating their bodies? Do you christianize
them unless you first civilize ? Can you make them
peaceable, virtuous and moral without clothing them,

feeding them, sheltering them? When their naked bodies are shivering with cold, dripping with rain, when they are roaming the forest and the shore, ignorant of where their next meal is to come from, when they are living the lives of beasts, must they not have the thoughts of beasts? If my boys are bound out to hard work among rough companions will their morals be as good as they would be with good influences? If they are raised on the street will the chances be in favor of their making good citizens? Do rich men's boys steal? Do rich men's daughters become castaways? Is not intelligence a source of virtue? And how intelligence without education, and how education without money? I tell you money means education, it means morality, it means great and good impulses, it means a noble ambition, it means an open path to virtue. I do not speak of *riches*, but of a decent independence. Enough to keep my family together—to help them fight the battles of the world with the advantage on their side. Now they must be turned adrift to buffet, weak and single-handed, with the billows that are hard enough to bear with all the aids humanity can gather. Oh! I have sinned against my own flesh and blood—Sinned!—Sinned!—Sinned!"

And with a gasp the sick man fell back exhausted, and spoke no more. He lay as in a deathly stupor till night and then he died.

The good clergyman quit his bedside in a profound study. He pondered over a new line of thought for days. Here was a practical, real, startlingly real difficulty not mentioned in his books. Here was a new duty he had never dreamed of; and here was a new remorse for its neglect—a remorse terrible enough to shut out all else from a dying man's thoughts.

For days he made no mention of the subject, either in conversation or otherwise,—he made no allusion to it in the funeral sermon. But day and night, in long and solitary walks, and in the quiet of his study he pondered over the problem. And meanwhile he watched the family of the deceased until he saw the dying prophecy come true. Homeless, penniless, now almost friendless, they were scattered to live by bitter drudgery, or still more bitter dependence.

The clergyman was an honest man; he did not close his mind to the convincing logic of facts, but he followed straight on down the vista of thought opened up before him till he had found his own duty, and then he fulfilled that duty as it appeared to him.

He announced on a sabbath morning, two weeks afterward that he would lecture that evening on

"The sin of dying poor."

As may well be imagined his congregation were astonished at the topic and the elders thought of remonstrating. Still when evening came the church was crowded.

But those who came to laugh soon became serious. Never had the minister conducted the exercises so solemnly and impressively. As he stood up to commence his sermon his countenance was grave and pale, and his voice had an intense, earnest, yet fearfully calm tone, that riveted the attention.

"From the bedside of the dying, from the wrestling of prayer, from the meditations of the closet, from the visits to the alms-house and the homes of the poor, I have lately learned a lesson—It is that it is a sin to die poor.

The sin may have its palliations, its excuses in exceptional cases, but it still is a wrong against God and man. A wrong against man, because it is man's duty to the world to leave it better than he found it. And to leave it better than he found it he must add to the common stock of the world's wealth. For the world's wealth represents its civilization, its intelligence, its industry, its energy, its refinement, its means of self-improvement, its elevation above the savage and the brute. It is its capital, enabling it to overcome the obstacles of nature, the weaknesses of humanity, the depravity of ignorance, and the temptations of poverty.

"The outcry against money is unjust and unwise. It is not money but the inordinate love of it that is the root of all evil. Money, itself, as a means, is a proper object of pursuit to all,—more, it should give a glow of satisfaction to all who possess it, for the quantity of it is a measure of one of the dimensions of a man's usefulness.

"Times are changed from two thousand years ago. Then brute force ruled the world. Capital, wealth, money, were limited, almost unknown and little valued. Civilization was in a low state, and so the financial question was a trifling one. Men had simple habits, and, therefore, their wants were simple, and it was just as well so, because their knowledge was limited in proportion, and their power likewise.

"After those times the world progressed, till inventive force and skill · began to control all else. Since then advance has been by long strides till now it has become one immense bound after another so that we can almost feel the earth tremble beneath us. Now, capital is the accumulated force of all the labors of past generations. Now, capital draws all things else to it and with it. Capital rules the nations, decides wars, makes people freemen or slaves, wise or ignorant, powerful or weak. Knowledge is power, but capital is a greater power, for it controls knowledge and makes it its servant.—Do you wish to do good? Are you poor? Your hands are tied.—Do you wish to protect yourselves from a private wrong? Do you wish to put down a pub-lte evil? Put money in thy purse. So has God willed it, that we must work with his instruments. So did Paul mean when he said: 'Be diligent in business,' "

Thus the preacher continued, drawing from the Bible, history and every-day life, sledge-hammer illustrations of his novel pulpit theme. We shall not undertake to repeat his sermon in full. The effect would be lost without the unusual, almost startling solemnity of his tone, showing the depth of the new conviction which, after such long struggles. filled his heart.

Finally he reached a new branch of the subject. He had been speaking of duty to God and to fellow men. Suddenly he dropped his voice to a sadder tone, and said:

"Above all, beyond all. to die poor is a sin to your families. To the helpless children you have brought into the world you owe protection, support, education and good influences. To the devoted wife whom you have taken when a blooming girl and left a helpless mother. with a mother's care and a mother's weaknesses, you owe support by your marriage vow. Toil. labor. self denial and economy of strength may be called for in the task. But you owe all these, for. 'If a man provide not for his own, especially for those of his own house, he hath denied the faith and is worse than an infidel.' Until you are able to build up a reservoir of property which will sustain your families at death, your duty is to insure your lives. Do so and you will have the sweet consciousness of having done your duty. You must do this if it is to be said of you, ' I have been young and now I am old; yet never have I seen the righteous man forsaken, nor his seed begging bread.' Your lives will thus be made happier and your death-beds sweeter.

" With the full sense of what I am saying, as the fruit of deliberate reflection, I repeat to you, my hearers, that Life Insurance is a Christian's duty. ' The good man leaveth an inheritance. And I know that he who dies with his family about him, leaving no inheritance, will condemn himself worse than I can condemn him.' "

Then he described the death-bed of the dying neighbor with all its harrowing remorses. There was not a dry eye in the audience. The congregation broke up with choking throats, and downcast, tearful eyes. As they walked home, husbands clasped the hands of their wives, and wives pressed the arms of their husbands as they mutually vowed to devote themselves thenceforward to a new duty.

Life Under a Cloud.

IN the same street of the same country town, and
directly opposite the unfortunate family described in our last paper, there lived another
family who were a perfect contrast to the former.

They were as painstaking, economical and serious
as the others had been gay and extravagant. The
father was the hardest working man in the neighborhood, the earliest and latest of all at his trade
of carpenter, carrying the heaviest timbers and doing willingly the most dangerous or difficult jobs
which the others shirked. Mornings and evenings
he toiled on his little lot, jumping from one task to
another without taking time to straighten himself
up, and any summer evening when it was not pitch
dark the belated passer by could hear his hoe click-
ing against the stones of his corn or potato patch
till midnight. His bent back and stiffened knees
had become a standing joke in the village; but
that never troubled him, for he never "wasted *his*
time loafing in stores or chatting on street corners."
He had "no time for such follies"; scarcely time
even to go to the polls on election days. His calen-

dar contained no holidays. And even Sundays was
an unwelcome break to his labors; though it cer-
tainly was no break to the current of his thoughts.
But Sunday evenings he retired unusually early to
secure a good start on Monday morning for the all
important week's labor.

It was not always so. Time had been when he
was a universal favorite for his youthful gaiety and
ready sympathy with the joys and sorrows of those
around him. That was when he was a young man.
But when he fell in love with a prudent neighbor's
daughter, and the old folks insisted that they
should not marry until he had a nice sum of money
laid by, he and his betrothed resolved to comply
with the advice. And so he went to work in
earnest. He gave up one after another all his old
pleasures and bent himself body and soul to the
task. It took him five years to accomplish it.

Five long years to the poor girl, who often re-
pented of the plan. She grew pale and thin,
changing far faster than the years should have
changed her. Folks said the courtship had lasted
over long already; and so she felt. But the man's
industry increased with time. Labor, from being
a means, had become a fixed habit and almost the
sole purpose of his life. His mind had fed on nothing else for five years, and so it had grown according to the only food it had. He had become

a laboring machine and little else. His noble feel-
ings had been stifled so relentlessly that they seemed to be smothered out of existence. He seemed
to live for work ; and he even dreamed of it, when
he dreamt at all. He toiled as though there was a
remorseless fiend at his back, lashing him on to re-
newed operations. You would have said he be-
lieved that the primeval curse was a blessing, and
that the Bible ended there.

They married,—but very privately, to save fool-
ish expense. And partly for the same reason, partly because they had lost their taste for society, they
lived very privately. The old sunny cheerfulness,
the old fervor of trusting affection were all gone ;
and all their talk and planning now was about the
" main chance," the being " prudent, saving, economical," the " getting on " in life. And as little
children began to multiply around their melancholy
fireside, the parents saw new reasons for accumula-
ting a fortune. And still as the pile increased,
their desire for more increased and thus they always
felt poor ; and for all practical purposes they *were*
as poor as the most unfortunate of their neighbors.

The wife drudged from morning to night, in-
fluenced by the example of her husband, but in a
listless treadmill sort of a way, as though her heart
was not in it, nor in any thing else. Her sad eyes
seemed to say that life had no charms for her. Yet

she was unconscious of the fact. She seemed to
think she was fulfilling life's highest duties. Im-
perceptibly to herself the hardness of her hands
had worked inwards towards her heart, till that
had grown hard too.

The children were dull, palefaced, serious little
things, older than their years, perfectly ignorant of
what play meant. Love for their parents was an
idea they scarcely knew the meaning of, for the latter never took time to show them any affection, nor
indeed scarcely ever noticed them except to instill
into their minds some useful lesson of economy and
premature wisdom, or to severely reprove them for
some childish carelessness. In fact they scarcely
ever met their father except at meals, and these
they eat in hurried solemn silence; or winter evenings when he would study the market reports, and
deaths from the weekly paper, and fall asleep trying
to read something else.

Still their parents were proud of them. They
stood highest in their classes at school, and did not
tear or soil their clothes like the "shiftless children
over the way." They were advised not to associate
with these latter, but the advice was unnecessary,
for the two families could no more mix than oil
and water.

The mother would at rare intervals find time to
make a formal call upon some of the neighbors

whom she named "sensible people." But it was her particular recreation to attend all the funerals of the neighborhood, and often she would come back and say to her husband that the bereaved family would "have to come down now in their pride, and go to work like other people."

Sometimes she would congratulate herself that her children would reap the reward of all their efforts some day and be looked up to with respect by the "spendthrifts" opposite, who, she said, "put all they had on their backs, and then turned up their noses at their neighbors."

"Our children," she used to say to herself, "will not be kept with their noses to the grindstone as we have been." She little thought that the chances were ten to one that having been taught to grub so long they would never be anything else but grubbers all their lives, unless perhaps a very probable reaction should make them reckless and dissolute.

Fortunately for them and their parents, the investment in which three-fourths of the family savings were placed, and which had been always considered as safe as it was profitable, about this time failed from over speculation and a depression in business, Added to which the oldest child showed symptoms of softening of the brain, from over study at too youthful an age, and the father was rendered unfit for work by severe dyspepsia, which caused his mind to magnify all his misfortunes.

A temporary business shock would not have disturbed that iron heart; it would soon have been forgotten in the absorbing cares of a busy life. Death itself would have had no terrors for his mind, for he would have met it unflinchingly, in the proud conviction that he had done his duty and would leave his family provided for. But when a lingering disease took away his heart's idol—work—when he was forced in spite of himself to move around the place and the town doing nothing, when he was condemned for the first time in many years to *think*, then his mental powers began to free themselves from the fetters they had worn so long.

One morning he noticed the listless dull air of his children, as they crept fearfully to the table and silently off to school; he watched them as they sat at night poring over their books, their minds evidently "wool gathering" over their tedious task; he went up stairs and stood by their beds, and looked at their thin colorless faces as they slept, and a tear dropped from his eye for the first time for years. He retired slowly and thoughtfully down stairs, put their books and slates into the fire and walked out to the store to come back with his arms full of all the playthings he could find.

Then he went to work to teach his children how to play, how to fish, to boat, to climb, to gather flowers and nuts, and to use a fowling piece. He

went back to where he had left off in his old boyish
days and became young again for their sakes, not
knowing that he was learning as much from them as
they from him. When the summer and autumn had
passed, he found his children hearty and rugged as
they never had been before ; and himself, to his sur-
prise, a well man again.

He went to work with great reluctance. His wife
was astonished that he often took holidays now to
make excursions with the children or to take the
whole family on visits to their friends. Books and
papers made their appearance at the house ; reading,
games, children's gatherings, pleasant chats with the
neighbors occupied every evening, and cheerful conversation and ready smiles, and a warm interest in
all the concerns of the family and of the village
marked every idle moment of the day. The glow
returned to the cheeks of the wife, and one day she
said to the husband.

" Tell me, how is it everything is so different.
Now you find time to look after other people's interest and happiness, and your mind is no longer
wrapped up in your own business matters. And,
oh, we are all so much happier than we used to be !
But what has changed your views? Are your children provided for in case of your death ? You seem
to love them more than ever, and I know you cannot
have forgotten them ! "

"I have forgotten nothing," was the reply. "But
I have learned that we have all been leading a mis-
taken life. While I live I can support you all com-
fortably. The only fear that haunted me day and
night, that drove me on to make a slave of myself
and slaves of the whole famlly, was the dread of my
sudden death, which might leave you unprovided
for. But I have lately learned a better way, a way
that wonld have made us all happier in days gone
by if I had known it sooner. Henceforward I shall
live like a man and no longer like a beast of burden.
Can you not guess the secret of it? Here it is—
he went to his desk and drew out *A Life Insurance
Policy*.

COMPARATIVE LIST

OF

Assets and Death Losses.

The following table proves how the Standard is in advance of almost all other companies in two most important points of all connected with Life Insurance. That is, *its Losses are less* in proportion and *its Assets are greater;* thus making insurance in it the cheapest and the safest.

	Ratio of Losses in 1869 to mean Amount at Risk.	Ratio of Assets to Liabilities.
STANDARD, . .	**0.54**	**205**
Ætna	0.94	128
American, ...	1.22	135
Atlas, St. Louis, . . .	0.72	150
Berkshire, . . .	0.76	113
Brooklyn, ...	0.73	114
Charter Oak, . .	1.03	126
Connecticut Mut. . . .	0.93	155
Continental, H'd, . .	0.78	161
Economical. . . .	0.93	148
Equitable, . .	0.96	100–120
Excelsior, ...	0.58	154
Germania, . . .	1.05	127
Globe, ...	0.67	113
Guardian, ...	0.99	121
Hahnemann, ...	0.65	167
Home, ...	0.85	119

John Hancock,	1.01	121
Knickerbocker,	1.23	125
Manhattan,	0.98	142
Massachusetts	1.05	111
Mutual, N. Y.,	0 89	100–120
Mutual Benefit,	0.96	121
Mut. Protection,	1.02	100–120
National Vt.	0.87	151
N. England Mut.	1.03	107
M. Jersey Mut.	1.04	142
New York,	0.80	122
North American,	0.97	113
North Western,	0.79	117
Penn. Mutual,	0.85	111
Phœnix,	0 58	100–120
Provident,	0 69	159
Security,	0.63	118
State Mutual of Worcester,	1.10	117
St. Louis,	1.27	106
Travelers,	0.86	182
Union Mutual of Maine,	0.70	127
United States,	1.22	140
Universal,	0.74	138
Washington,	0.71	112
Wid's and Orphans,	0.93	123
World,	0.78	169
Piedmont and Arlington,	60	138

Board of Trustees.

HON. E. D. MORGAN, U. S. Senator.
HON GEO. OPDYKE, late Mayor of the City of N. Y., President.
GOUVR. M. WILKINS, Castle Hill, Westchester.
LE GRAND LOCKWOOD, Lockwood & Co.. Bankers.
F. A. PALMER, President of Broadway National Bank.
WM. H. GUION, Williams & Guion.
J. B. CORNELL, J. B. & W. W. Cornell.
RICHARD LATHERS, President Great Western Ins. Co.
E. H. LUDLOW, E. H. Ludlow & Co
HENRY M. TABER, C. C. & H. M. Taber
I. VAN ANDEN, Proprietor Brooklyn Eagle.
WM. PEET, Miller, Peet & Opdyke.
JAMES L. DAWES, Vice-President.
JNO. G. MEIGGS, Merchant.
S. T. SCRANTON, President Oxford Iron Co.
C. ASHWORTH, Banker.
HON. THEO. F. RANDOLPH, Governor of New Jersey
THOMAS INGHAM, Metal Merchant.
WILSON G. HUNT, late W. G. Hunt & Co.
EUGENE KELLY, Eugene Kelly & Co.
JAMES C. HOLDEN, Iron Merchant.
TREDWELL KETCHAM, Banker.
BENJ. H. FIELD.
A. BRAYTON BALL. M. D.

THE STANDARD

LIFE INSURANCE COMPANY,

202 BROADWAY.

NEW YORK.

———◆━●━◆———

President: Vice-President:
GEORGE OPDYKE.   JAMES L. DAWES.

Secretary and Actuary:
CHARLES W. OPDYKE.

Ass't Secretary:
WM. A. CHILDS.

Medical Examiner:
A. BRAYTON BALL, M. D.

PURELY MUTUAL.   ALL PROFITS TO POLICY
HOLDERS.

No Injustice to the Insured in case of Non-Payment of Premiums.

ASSETS DOUBLE ITS LIABILITIES.

www.ingramcontent.com/pod-product-compliance
Lightning Source LLC
Chambersburg PA
CBHW032033090426
42733CB00031B/1203

* 9 7 8 3 3 3 7 3 4 0 5 2 0 *